754

W9-CZS-640

SURVIVOR

DR. JERRI NIELSEN
Cheating Death
in Antarctica

Scott P. Werther

HIGH
interest
books

Children's Press®
A Division of Scholastic Inc.
New York / Toronto / London / Auckland / Sydney
Mexico City / New Delhi / Hong Kong
Danbury, Connecticut

In memory of Mary Jean Fenzel

Book Design: Christopher Logan
Contributing Editor: Matt Pitt

Photo Credits: Cover, back cover © National Science Foundation; pp. 4, 25, 36 © Josh Landis/National Science Foundation; p. 8, 31, 32, 40 © AP/Wide World Photos; pp. 13, 14, 39 © Melanie Conner/National Science Foundation; p. 19 © Lester Lefkowitz/Corbis; p. 20 © Galen Rowell/Corbis; p. 27 © Corbis; p. 28 © Roger Ressmeyer/Corbis; p. 35 © Alexander Colhoun/National Science Foundation

Library of Congress Cataloging-in-Publication Data

Werther, Scott P.
    Dr. Jerri Nielsen : Cheating Death in Antarctica / Scott P. Werther.
    p. cm.—(Survivor)
    Summary: Recounts Dr. Jerri Nielsen's struggle to survive cancer while in Antarctica.
    Includes bibliographical references and index.
    ISBN 0-516-24331-4 (lib. bdg.) — ISBN 0-516-27870-3 (pbk.)
    1. Nielsen, Jerri—Health—Juvenile literature. 2. Breast—Cancer—Patients—Antarctica—Biography—Juvenile literature. 3. Women physicians—Antarctica—Biography—Juvenile literature.[1. Nielsen, Jerri. 2. Physicians. 3. Cancer—Patients. 4. Women—Biography. 5. Antarctica. 6. Survival.] I. Title: Doctor Jerri Nielsen. II. Title: Cheating death in Antarctica. III. Title. IV. Series.

RC280.B8N545 2003
362.1'96994'0092—dc21

2003001605

Contents

Introduction

Dr. Jerri Nielsen had seen, up close, the damage that cancer could do. She knew how quickly the disease could spread inside a healthy body. If a victim didn't get the right kind of medical help in time, that person's life could be over.

However, she never thought she would get that close to cancer. In the spring of 1999, Dr. Nielsen, age forty-seven, found a lump in her breast. She was worried. She suspected the lump was cancer. If she'd been in the United States, she wouldn't have been as concerned about her discovery. She was in Antarctica, though—thousands of miles from family, friends, and hospitals.

Before flying to Antarctica, Dr. Nielsen was warned that it was "the highest, driest, coldest, windiest, and emptiest place on earth." This warning proved to be true. Temperatures can dip far below zero. For eight months, there is no way

 For several months, Dr. Jerri Nielsen's hopes of survival seemed as bleak as the icy landscape where she was living.

to leave the continent. The rough weather prevents planes from flying in or out.

Dr. Nielsen didn't have the proper equipment to find out whether or not she actually had cancer. To make matters worse, she was the only person there with medical training. If it became necessary to operate and remove the lump, she would have to do it herself. The lump was growing fast, doubling in size every two weeks. The pain from it was increasing. The conditions at the South Pole were only growing worse. Dr. Nielsen wasn't giving up, though. She was determined to fight through each dark day of the long winter ahead.

Each year, people interested in science and exploration work in the frigid conditions of Antarctica (shown in this map). Jerri Nielsen was the doctor in charge of everyone's health at the Amundsen-Scott Station.

Atlantic Ocean

ANTARCTICA

Pacific Ocean

✚
SOUTH POLE — AMUNDSEN - SCOTT STATION (U.S.A)

Indian Ocean

NEW ZEALAND

The new home for Polies should be completed by 2005. It will feature faster computers and newer equipment—things that Dr. Nielsen was forced to go without.

One

Cold Comforts

Every year, groups of people spend periods of time at the Amundsen-Scott South Pole Station in Antarctica. Most visitors stay during Antarctica's summer months. Since Antarctica is in the Southern Hemisphere, however, its seasons are the opposite of those in the Northern Hemisphere. The summer months in Antarctica are the winter months in the Northern Hemisphere. Once February rolls around, most people leave the South Pole. The South Pole Station becomes closed to new visitors. However, a small crew of about forty scientists, electricians, and construction workers "winter over." This brave crew calls one another "Polies."

Polies study many things about the conditions in Antarctica. They work in areas such as marine life, astronomy, and global warming. Once winter is at its worst, temperatures dip below -100°F (-73°C). The station shuts down.

For eight months, no airplanes can fly to the station. Their wheels would freeze to the ground within minutes. The extreme cold would also harden the plane's fuel. These same conditions prevent people from leaving the station. No matter how sick they might get, Polies must remain at the station until winter ends. Each year, the health of every Polie depends on a single doctor.

Did You Know?

Whenever Dr. Nielsen went outside, she wore six layers of clothing. These layers included a fleece jumpsuit and jacket, overalls, and a goose-down parka.

Dr. Jerri Nielsen was the doctor for the 1998-1999 "winter over" crew. Why had she agreed to do this? She had just gone through a difficult year.

After a painful divorce, her three teenaged children were living with her ex-husband. This turn of events had left her very depressed. She was constantly thinking about her children.

Dr. Nielsen had faced struggles before. During one of her first days as a medical student, she had been driving to the hospital. Suddenly, a speeding car plowed into her from behind. The accident left Dr. Nielsen with terrible back pain. Dr. Nielsen said that the accident taught her a valuable lesson: "That a person could lose everything in an instant." Though she was in tremendous pain, she managed to finish her education.

However, she'd never gone through this kind of *emotional* pain before. When the position for a doctor in Antarctica opened up, Dr. Nielsen signed up. She felt that starting an adventure would be the best way for her to clear her mind from all the sadness. Her family supported her decision. Dr. Nielsen's mom knew the months ahead would be challenging. Yet she reminded her daughter, "You've always been a survivor."

At Home in the Dome

Dr. Nielsen arrived in Antarctica in late November. Hauling heavy bags of clothes behind her, she entered the Dome for the first time. The Dome is a large aluminum building 165 feet (50.3 meters) tall and 55 feet (16.8 m) wide. The Dome is not heated. The temperature is almost the same inside the Dome as it is outside. On the summer day when Dr. Nielsen entered the Dome for the first time, it was -35°F (-37°C).

Inside the Dome was a cluster of smaller buildings. Power generators heated these smaller buildings. Dr. Nielsen's home was called the Biomed building. It was where she would live and treat patients.

Dr. Nielsen struggled to adjust to Antarctica's rough conditions. The altitude of Antarctica is higher than any other continent. The high altitude made Dr. Nielsen feel dizzy and disoriented. She often lost track of time. Living in high altitudes can even cause brain damage. Also, the sun never sets during an Antarctic summer. Polies often have trouble telling the difference between day and night.

Fun Out of the Sun

For entertainment, Polies spend time in the gym or in the TV lounge. To keep in touch with friends and family back home, Polies mainly use e-mail. E-mail at the Pole works only by satellite. Dr. Nielsen used the Internet to tell loved ones about her life at the Pole. She had no idea that the Internet would someday save her life.

Over the last thirty years, South Pole snowdrifts have managed to bury parts of the Dome.

While Dr. Nielsen's stay at the South Pole was terrifying, it had moments of beauty, too. Looking out of the Viper telescope (above) gave her crystal-clear views of the deepest regions of space.

Two

A Difficult Discovery

A few weeks after Dr. Nielsen arrived, a call came in on her radio. She was told to report to the base immediately. At the moment she got the call, Dr. Nielsen was studying a telescope that probed into the deepest reaches of space. Since the telescope was only a quarter mile (.4 kilometers) from the base, she decided to walk back. All of a sudden, a snowmobile pulled up next to her. Dr. Nielsen could tell by the scared look in the driver's eyes that someone's life might be in danger. She jumped on.

A man at the base had collapsed in a seizure. When Dr. Nielsen got to him, he was awake, but very confused. He would be fine. However, he would need to be sent away from the base as soon as possible. There was too much risk he'd have another seizure. Once the base closed for winter, he'd have no way of getting out.

A Lucky Woman

The incident reminded Dr. Nielsen that she was a fundamental part of the station. She was the only one who knew how to use the station's medical equipment—even though she wasn't familiar with a lot of it. Most of the equipment was old or out of order. The X-ray machine barely worked. Some of the machinery had been made in the 1950s. The Polies would be moving into a new dome in 2005. Its equipment would be modern. Unfortunately, that wouldn't do Dr. Nielsen's patients any good in 1999. Still, she was glad to be helping others, and glad for the adventure. Her brother Scott e-mailed Dr. Nielsen just before Christmas, reminding her that she was lucky to be there. "Enjoy and savor every minute of it," he wrote.

Winter Hits Hard

By early February, everyone who wasn't wintering over had left the Pole. On February 4, the doors to the Dome were sealed. It was -55°F (-48°C) inside the Dome. Yet the worst of the cold was on its way. For the next eight months, the Polies would be completely dependent on their power generators. If the generators failed, the smaller, heated buildings would become as cold as the Dome. Survival would be nearly impossible.

The Polies had to face that problem only a few weeks later. Several of the power generators

Did You Know?

The South Pole receives less than an inch of snow every year. However, the snow never melts.

started smoking. Everyone was frightened. Luckily, one of the Polies was trained to fix this problem. John "Big John" Penney, Dr. Nielsen's best friend at the Pole, took charge. Big John was responsible for fixing mechanical problems. He discovered that an important part of the machinery had sprung a leak. The crew quickly repaired the leak and avoided a crisis. Still, it was a grim reminder to the Polies of just how vulnerable they were.

Discovering the Lump

In early March, Dr. Nielsen's personal crisis began. She was in her bed, reading a book. While she read, her hand brushed against her chest. It hit a small, hard lump.

This discovery wasn't a complete shock. Dr. Nielsen had fibrocystic breasts. This non-fatal condition sometimes caused small lumps to form in the breast. In the past, Dr. Nielsen's lumps always went away within weeks.

If the lump persisted, it could indicate cancer. However, it was too early to be alarmed. Shortly

Many experts in medicine feel that mammograms can help detect breast cancer at its earliest stages.

before leaving for Antarctica, she had a mammogram. A mammogram is an examination performed by doctors to check patients for breast cancer. Dr. Nielsen had checked out fine.

Still, it was hard not to worry. Without other doctors or reliable medical equipment around, a cancerous lump on the South Pole could be a death sentence.

She decided not to tell anyone. The other Polies might panic if they knew their only doctor's health was in question.

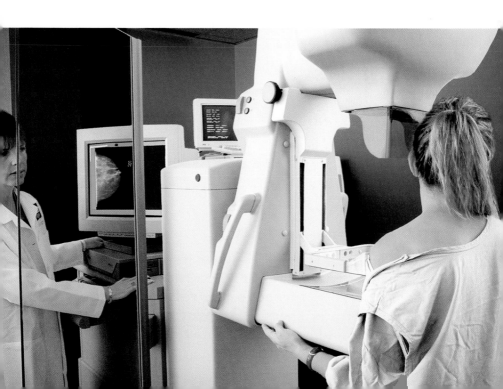

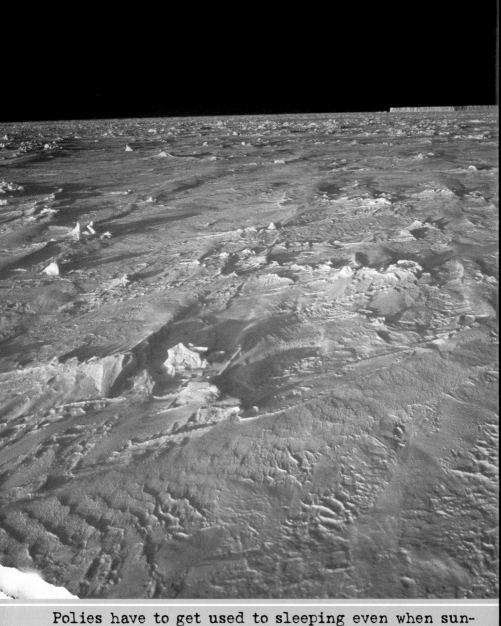

Polies have to get used to sleeping even when sunlight surrounds them. This photograph of Antarctica was taken about midnight!

Three

Fighting an Unseen Enemy

Darkness Sets In

On March 22, the sun set in the South Pole for the first time in four months. Now that it was gone, it would stay dark for the next six months.

Just as the sky was darkening, so was Jerri Nielsen's mood. The lump hadn't disappeared. In fact, it had become larger. To make matters worse, another lump was forming underneath the first one. She knew that cancer wasn't the only explanation. Yet she also knew that if she did have cancer, she might not survive the winter.

Conditions were worsening, both inside and outside the Dome. Dr. Nielsen noticed ice patches on the ceiling of the Biomed building and inside one of her offices' storage cabinets. The extreme cold had even froze the medical equipment used to treat hypothermia! The air was so dry that Dr. Nielsen woke up each morning with her tongue stuck to her mouth.

The Polies faced other challenges as well. Now that the Polies were cast in darkness, even walking outside the Dome presented problems. In the past, some Polies had fallen into cracks in the ice. These cracks could go down for hundreds of feet. Finally, Dr. Nielsen worried that the high altitude might badly affect her thinking.

Despite the danger and difficulty, Dr. Nielsen had grown to love her life at the Pole. People listened to and helped one another. Every Polie worked hard to keep the station working. They all worked together to keep one another safe. Dr. Nielsen thought that if she were going to die in Antarctica, at least the last year of her life would be one of her best.

Time to Tell

By early June, a swelling under Dr. Nielsen's right arm was causing her tremendous pain. She decided it was time to let the others know what was going on. She wanted the Polies to be prepared for the possibility that their doctor was becoming the sickest patient.

The first Polie Dr. Nielsen told was the man who ran the base, Mike Masterman. Masterman didn't see the situation as hopeless. He wondered if they might be able to cut out the tumor. He told her to e-mail doctors in the United States to get their advice. Nielsen did just that.

In their replies, the doctors said they were against Dr. Nielsen attempting to operate on herself. They said she would only be able to use one hand, making it impossible to remove the entire tumor. She might also pass out during the surgery and bleed to death. She could even get a serious infection after the operation. Finally—due to the altitude and temperature at the Pole—her surgical wounds might not heal properly.

The doctors agreed that she should use a needle to get a sample of the fluid inside the tumor. Removing fluids from the body this way is called a biopsy. By examining this fluid, Dr. Nielsen could determine if the tumor was cancerous.

Dr. Nielsen met with the other Polies, to let them know what was happening. They immediately suggested ways to get her out of Antarctica, and into proper medical care. They weren't willing to let one of their own die.

On June 22, Dr. Nielsen performed the biopsy. She chose her friend, Paul "Pakman" Kindl, to help her use a needle to get the fluid out. Although Pakman was an electrician, he had trained with a team to help out in medical emergencies.

The biopsy was a long, painful process. Dr. Nielsen could only numb herself with an ice cube. When Pakman inserted the needle into her breast, it hit a hard mass. Pakman tried several times to draw fluid from the lump. Unfortunately, he could not. This meant the tumor was probably cancerous.

Inside the Dome, Dr. Nielsen's condition rapidly became worse. Part of her wondered if she'd ever see the sunlight again.

Leaning on Friends

Dr. Nielsen's friends tried to keep her spirits up. They got her out of bed when she was depressed and brushed her hair. A friend of hers from the United States had told a doctor in Indiana about Dr. Nielsen's condition. The doctor, Kathy Miller, specialized in breast cancer. In e-mails, Dr. Miller asked Dr. Nielsen a series of questions. She wanted to see if she could figure out the best treatment in case the lump was cancerous.

To help his friend, Big John had written to congressmen and senators in the United States. In his letters, he pleaded for medical equipment to be air dropped to the Dome. Suddenly, Dr. Nielsen's

private problem was becoming a very public concern. Once her difficulty was heard about, her story would be in newspapers and on television throughout the United States. Dr. Nielsen wanted her family to hear the news directly from her. On June 15, she called her family in Ohio to break the news. Dr. Nielsen's family stayed calm, trying to reassure her that things would take a turn for the better.

She appreciated everyone's love and support. However, she knew it would take a lot of work, determination—and luck—for her to survive this long winter.

The weaker that Dr. Nielsen became, the stronger the support from her fellow Polies grew. Their concern for her carried her through her crisis.

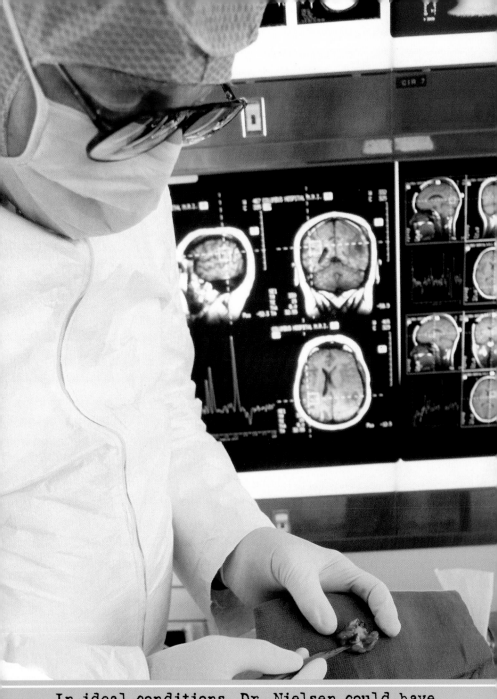

In ideal conditions, Dr. Nielsen could have had a trained doctor perform the breast biopsies. Unfortunately, she was forced to rely on friends who had little training. She was both patient and doctor.

Four

Beating the Cancer

Dr. Miller told Dr. Nielsen in e-mails that she would need to go through another biopsy. This one would involve taking a tissue sample from the lump. They planned on using video to broadcast the tissue samples back to the United States. Dr. Miller was going to try to save the life of a patient 11,600 miles (18,668 km) away.

The Polies did everything they could to help. One of the Polies, Walt, had once been trained as an army medic. He would help with the biopsy. To practice the delicate procedure, Walt and Dr. Nielsen poked needles into fruits and vegetables.

Since she needed to watch the biopsy, Dr. Nielsen couldn't take drugs to dull the pain of the procedure. The drugs would cloud her mind, and she wouldn't be able to pay close attention. They again numbed her skin with ice cubes. Meanwhile, other Polies were setting up a video connection. They would beam images of the biopsy to a team of doctors in the United States. The biopsy had to be performed at the exact time that the communication satellites were in contact with the Pole. It was a very small window of time.

Walt inserted a large needle into Dr. Nielsen. The needle drew tissue from the lump. This tissue was then put on slides and videotaped. Finally, the slide images were beamed to the United States through a special video-microscope. This would give Dr. Miller the information she needed to examine the mass.

Relief From the Sky

While Dr. Miller examined the images, an airdrop of medical supplies was being planned. Planes would fly over the station in early July and drop off supplies. This mission would be risky. There was no sunlight at the Pole. Previous airdrops

Desperately trying to beat the clock, the U.S. Air Force airdropped medical equipment and supplies to help Dr. Nielsen through her situation. ▶

took place when the moon was full. Unfortunately, they wouldn't have another full moon until late July. If they waited that long, Dr. Nielsen's chances of survival would worsen.

Meanwhile, back in the United States, Dr. Nielsen's story was receiving national attention. Anchorperson Dan Rather reported the problems at the Pole on the evening news, although he didn't refer to Dr. Nielsen by name. Newspaper articles about the airdrop began to appear throughout the country.

On July 9, only twenty-two hours before the airdrop, a power generator caught on fire. Dr. Nielsen had never been more scared in her life. If the Polies were forced to abandon the Dome, it would put Dr. Nielsen's chances of survival at an even greater risk. Finally, a call came over the radio from Big John. Once again, he and the other Polies were able to fix the problem.

Late the next night, a C-141 Starlifter cargo plane buzzed in the distance. Burning barrels marked the spot where the plane should drop its precious cargo. It was -92°F (-69°C) outside. The plane circled twice and dropped off several

packages before flying off. Polies rushed to get the packages before the materials inside the boxes froze. One package took over an hour to find. Everyone was celebrating when they finally made it back to the station. There was mail, fresh fruit and vegetables, and best of all, medical supplies for Dr. Nielsen. The contents in these boxes could save their friend's life.

The boxes didn't just contain survival items. Dr. Nielsen received a few extra gifts. They included silk flowers, personal letters, and get-well cards. Her battle for survival was touching people thousands of miles away.

Chemotherapy

On July 22, Dr. Nielsen was reading e-mails from the doctors back in the United States. One of them confirmed her worst fears: She definitely had cancer. It was aggressive and growing fast. By now the tumor was about the size of a hen's egg.

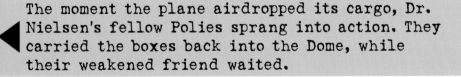

The moment the plane airdropped its cargo, Dr. Nielsen's fellow Polies sprang into action. They carried the boxes back into the Dome, while their weakened friend waited.

Dr. Nielsen's last hope was to immediately start chemotherapy. Chemotherapy is a medical process of using chemicals and drugs to kill diseased cells. The drugs can help shrink a tumor. However, they often cause bad side effects in their patients, such as fatigue and hair loss.

A few days later, the Polies had a video conference with Dr. Miller in Indiana. Dr. Miller gave them instructions on how to administer the chemotherapy drugs. The drugs made Dr. Nielsen woozy. She passed out a few times. Each time she did, her life was in the hands of Polies, who had no professional medical training.

Barely Holding Up

Dr. Nielsen's supply of hope was running low. The chemotherapy was making her throw up. At times, she wondered why she should bother taking the drugs at all. Fellow Polies, her family, and Dr. Miller all kept supporting her when her spirits sank.

To ease the embarrassment Dr. Nielsen felt when her hair started falling out, the Polies shaved their heads in an act of support.

In early August, the first faint hints of the sun appeared on the horizon. By that time, Dr. Nielsen's tumor had begun to shrink. She started to see patients again. Dr. Nielsen continued her chemotherapy throughout August. The side effects were rough. Dr. Nielsen felt tired for long stretches of times. When she brushed her hair, large clumps of it would come out. She and the other Polies tried to make the best of this sad setback. They held a head-shaving party! Several of the Polies had knitted caps. They gave these

to Dr. Nielsen to keep her head warm. The kindness of the Polies kept Dr. Nielsen's spirits up.

Desperate Acts

Even though the treatment seemed to be working, Dr. Nielsen wasn't free from danger. The tumor became painful again in early September.

The South Pole station is on 9,000 feet (2,373 m) of ice, 9,300 feet (2,835 m) above sea level. Even though it's flat, it's as high as the Austrian Alps in Europe.

Once again, she had serious doubts she would survive. To make matters worse, the tumor began to grow again. By the end of the month, Dr. Nielsen's situation had become critical. If she didn't get help soon, there was no way she would survive.

Acting quickly, Dr. Miller switched Dr. Nielsen to a stronger form of chemotherapy. Stronger drugs had been included in the airdrop only as a last resort. Now there was no time to waste. The tumor was doubling in size every two weeks.

Dr. Miller also contacted the Antarctic Support Associates (ASA). This group was in charge of scheduling flights to and from the South Pole. Normally, the ASA tried to wait until October 25 before allowing planes to land at the Pole. It was risky to let them come any sooner. However, Dr. Miller arranged a rescue mission for her patient nine days earlier. It would add some risk to fly to the Pole early. For Dr. Nielsen though, those nine days might mean the difference between life and death.

Safe and Sound

The first rescue mission took off on October 15. Terrible conditions forced the plane to turn back, however. The next morning's weather wasn't much better. Still, temperatures were expected to warm up just a bit. This time, the plane would land at the Pole. When it landed, the Polies would only have a few minutes to get Dr. Nielsen onboard.

Dr. Nielsen was exhausted from the drugs and the anxiety. She said goodbye to a couple of friends. Big John raced Dr. Nielsen to the plane on a snowmobile. She was so weak that she couldn't climb the stairs to the plane. Big John lifted her in and said a quick, but loving, goodbye. The U.S. National Guard plane took off for the blue skies above.

Dr. Nielsen was flown first to New Zealand, and then on to the United States. Her family was overjoyed to see her. They hugged her again and again. Her brothers presented a heaping plate of fresh produce. Gratefully, she wolfed down lettuce and green peppers. Within a couple of days, Dr. Nielsen was in Indiana with Dr. Miller.

The cancerous lump was removed from Dr. Nielsen's breast. For a number of weeks she was sicker than she'd been while at the Pole.

The recovery was long and difficult. Eventually, Dr. Nielsen's hair grew back in. Her strength returned. The help of friends, as well as her own determination, had carried her to another day. In spite of everything, Dr. Nielsen still considers living at the South Pole "the most wonderful thing that's ever happened to me."

Even after Dr. Nielsen was rescued from the heart of Antarctica, she still wasn't sure if the cancer would claim her life.

She tries to live her life to the fullest. She's even tried new adventures. Dr. Nielsen and a fellow Polie spent a week in Oklahoma looking for tornadoes. Some people might have been too fearful to attempt such a thing—not Dr. Nielsen. She had already weathered the most difficult storm of all—a chilling brush with death.

Dr. Nielsen's courageous battle with cancer earned her the respect of American leaders such as Senator Hillary Rodham Clinton and former president Bill Clinton.

TIMELINE

In 1998, Jerri Nielsen decided to accept an exciting opportunity. She would "winter over" at the South Pole. Her job was to serve as the doctor for all of the workers at the Amundsen-Scott Station. Although Dr. Nielsen enjoyed her early days in Antarctica, she soon learned shocking news: she had breast cancer. She was the only one with medical training. The medical equipment at the station was outdated, or sometimes faulty. Worst of all, there was no way she could leave Antarctica for several months. Thanks to her friends' support, and her own determination, Dr. Nielsen beat the odds and overcame cancer.

November 1998: Dr. Nielsen arrives in Antarctica.

December: Dr. Nielsen has her first serious patient: a man with a seizure has to be sent off the base before the long winter begins.

February 4, 1999: The doors to the Dome are closed for the winter.

March 22: The sun sets for six months.

June 21: Tissue is taken from Dr. Nielsen's lump.

July 10: An airdrop of supplies arrived.

July 22: Dr. Nielsen finds out she definitely has cancer. She immediately begins chemotherapy.

Early September: The tumor doubles in size. Dr. Nielsen has serious doubts about whether or not she will survive the cancer.

October 16: Dr. Nielsen is rescued from the Pole.

NEW WORDS

altitude (**al**-ti-tood) the height of something above the ground

biopsy (**bye**-op-see) the removal and examination of tissue, cells, or fluids from a living body

cancer (**kan**-sur) a serious disease in which some cells in the body grow faster than normal cells and destroy healthy organs and tissues

chemotherapy (kee-moh-**ther**-uh-pee) the use of chemicals to kill diseased cells in cancer patients

cluster (**kluhss**-tur) to stand or grow close together

conference (**kon**-fur-uhnss) a formal meeting for discussing ideas and opinions

coordinate (koh-**or**-duh-nate) to organize activities or people so they all work together

disoriented (diss-**or**-ee-uhnt-ed) to have lost one's sense of time, place, or identity

essential (i-**sen**-shuhl) when something is really important and you cannot do without it

fibrocystic (fye-bruh-**sis**-tik) when parts of the body have fibrous tissue and cysts

hypothermia (hye-puh-**thur**-mee-uh) when a person's body temperature has become dangerously low

mammogram (**mam**-uh-gram) a test that scans a woman's breast to check for cancer

plummet (**pluh**-muht) to fall sharply and abruptly

rupture (**ruhp**-chur) to break open or to burst

savor (**say**-vur) to take great joy in something

seizure (**see**-zhur) sudden attack of illness, or a spasm

tumor (**too**-mur) an abnormal lump or mass in the body

vulnerable (**vuhl**-nur-uh-buhl) someone in a weak position who is likely to be hurt or damaged in some way

Billings, Henry. *Antarctica*. Chicago, IL
Scholastic Library Publishing, 1994.

McDonald, Kellie. *Antarctica*. Chicago, IL
Heinemann Library, 1997.

Nielsen, Dr. Jerri. *Ice Bound: A Doctor's
Incredible Battle for Survival at the South Pole*.
New York: Hyperion. 2001.

RESOURCES

Organizations

The National Science Foundation (NSF)
National Science Foundation
Office of Polar Programs
Room 755
4201 Wilson Boulevard
Arlington, VA 22230
Tel: (703) 292-8030
Fax: (703) 292-9081
http://www.nsf.gov/od/opp/support/southp.htm

RESOURCES

Web Sites

Everything on Antarctica

www.70south.com

This Web site features many articles on Antarctica. It provides constant updates from the continent.

United States Government Site

www.spole.gov

This site provides all the information on the Amundsen-Scott Station in Antarctica. You can even take a virtual tour of the Dome.

National Alliance of Breast Cancer Organizations

www.nabco.org

Find up-to-date facts and information on breast cancer, as well as important statistics.

INDEX

INDEX

About the Author

Scott P. Werther is an editor and freelance writer from Monkton, Maryland. He recommends that all readers spend some time in the outdoors.